M is for Mountain State

A West Virginia Alphabet

Written by Mary Ann McCabe Riehle and Illustrated by Laura J. Bryant

Sleeping Bear Press™

2395 South Huron Parkway, Suite 200
Ann Arbor, MI 48104
www.sleepingbearpress.com

Printed and bound in the United States.

15 14 13 12 11

Riehle, Mary Ann McCabe, 1959-
M is for Mountain State : a West Virginia alphabet / written by
Mary Ann McCabe Riehle ; illustrated by Laura J. Bryant.
p. cm.
ISBN-13: 978-1-58536-151-9
1. English language—Alphabet—Juvenile literature. 2. West Virginia—
Juvenile literature. I. Bryant, Laura J. II. Title.
F241.3.R54 2004
975.4—dc22   2004006279

To family and friends throughout the United States,
no matter which state you call home, you are close to my heart.

MARY ANN

❦

To all of my wonderful neighbors who have extended
generous amounts of good humor and friendship.

To the many trails I have walked in West Virginia where
each turn of the path reveals something new and beautiful.

LAURA

The awesome Allegheny Mountains are the tallest mountains in West Virginia. Also known as the Alleghenies, these mountains are located along the eastern border in the Appalachian Ridge and Valley Region. This is where you'll find Spruce Knob, the highest point in the state. Its peak is nearly 5,000 feet above sea level. Also, the Monongahela National Forest is located in the Allegheny Mountains.

Streams on the east side of the Allegheny Mountains flow to the Atlantic Ocean and those on the other side flow to the Gulf of Mexico.

Climb to the top of letter A.
Allegheny Mountains point the way
to a place that you can go
and admire the beauty down below.

What's the buzz about letter B
and the animals it features?
Black bears, birds, the honeybee,
and lots of other creatures.

B b

The forests and waters of West Virginia make a comfortable home for many types of animals. The black bear, the official state animal, lives in the forest where it can climb trees. Black bears are also able to swim. Weighing over 200 pounds, the adult black bear may be one of the largest animals in the forest.

In 1973, the same year the black bear was designated the state animal, the brook trout was named the state fish.

The state bird is the cardinal. The official state insect of West Virginia is the honeybee. The monarch butterfly was declared the state butterfly in 1995.

If you see the letter C
or a dome glistening in the sun,
you'll know you're in our capital,
the city of Charleston.

The golden dome of the capitol building is perhaps the first thing you'll see when arriving in Charleston. The dome is one of the many spectacular features of the building designed by architect Cass Gilbert. The building was completed in 1932. Hanging inside the capitol dome is a chandelier with over 10,000 crystals. The chandelier is cleaned every four years, just in time for a governor's inauguration.

Charleston was not originally the capital city. Wheeling served as West Virginia's first capital. The state legislature voted several times, changing the capital from Wheeling to Charleston and back again to Wheeling. Eventually the vote was put to the people of West Virginia and Charleston became the capital in 1885. Each time the location of the state capital changed, state archives and records were transferred by boat up and down the Ohio and Kanawha Rivers.

Drummers make a distinct sound.
Dirt is formed into a sacred mound.
These help us discover letter D
and our state's special ancestry.

The Native American Pow Wow, a celebration of heritage, is held each year near the South Charleston Mound, the second largest burial mound in West Virginia. Over 2,000 years ago, massive amounts of dirt were carried by basket to construct sacred burial mounds. This required the efforts of several generations and took more than 100 years to build. Moundsville, West Virginia is where Native Americans known as the Adena people built Grave Creek Mound. It is one of the largest burial mounds in the United States and the largest in West Virginia. This mound is made of nearly 60,000 tons of dirt. Artifacts discovered at these mounds help us to learn about the lives and customs of the Native Americans.

E e

Educators teach us about letter **E**,
like a man named Booker T.
And Eleanor Roosevelt gave us a sample
of how to educate by example.

Educator Booker Taliaferro Washington grew up in Malden, West Virginia.

After being freed from slavery, his family moved to Malden when he was nine years old. Booker T. valued learning and believed that education would help bring about equality. He became the founder of the Tuskegee Institute in Alabama. His autobiography, *Up from Slavery*, was published in 1901.

Eleanor Roosevelt, wife of President Franklin Roosevelt, was particularly interested in education and equal opportunity for all. She directed relief programs in West Virginia during the 1930s and the Great Depression.

Many people had housing provided by their employers but when rough economic times caused many companies to close, both their jobs and the company-provided homes were lost. Mrs. Roosevelt helped the unemployed find places to live. Some families were able to move to planned communities known as home-steads. Red House Farms was one of those communities. Its name was later changed to Eleanor, West Virginia to honor Mrs. Roosevelt's efforts.

BOOKER T. WASHINGTON

ELEANOR ROOSEVELT

Many state symbols are included in our flag's design. The state seal in the center of the flag is surrounded by the state flower, the rhododendron.

The state motto, *Montani Semper Liberi*, meaning "Mountaineers Are Always Free," appears at the bottom of the seal.

In the center a farmer and a miner are shown standing beside a rock. The date shown on the rock is the day that West Virginia became a state. During the early stages of the Civil War, Virginia seceded from the Union but those living in the western part of that state decided to form their own state. West Virginia became the 35th state by proclamation of President Lincoln on June 20, 1863.

F is for the Flag
        that tells a lot about our state.
It displays so many symbols
            that make West Virginia great.

Ff

G g

Glassware found on the dinner table, in a church window, or among a group of children playing marbles is likely to have been made in West Virginia. Light shines through stained glass from West Virginia in churches as grand as the Washington National Cathedral in our nation's capital.

If you've lost your marbles, factories in Parkersburg could easily replace them since nearly all of the glass marbles in America are made there.

The availability of natural gas needed to make glass, and the rivers and railroads needed to transport the finished products, made West Virginia a logical place for glassmaking to thrive.

Look through a window; take in the view.
Glass bottles, vases, and even marbles too.
It should be very clear to see
that Glass begins with letter G.

Harper's Ferry holds a place in history as the site of a raid on the United States arsenal that began events leading up to the Civil War. The raid was led by John Brown, an abolitionist, who wanted the weapons in the arsenal to arm a rebellion against slavery. Brown and his followers were captured by troops. He was convicted of treason and hung. Union soldiers later sang Brown's praises in song while some Southerners considered his actions an act of war.

Huntington was also home to Dr. Carter Woodson. He is considered the "Father of Black History." In 1926 he initiated what is now known as Black History Month.

Hillsboro is the birthplace of author Pearl S. Buck. In 1932 she won the Pulitzer Prize in fiction for her novel, *The Good Earth.* Six years later she was awarded the Nobel Prize in literature. Pearl S. Buck was the first woman in history to receive both literary awards.

Letter H happens to be for Historic towns—
one once raided by a man named Brown.
Huntington and Hillsboro too
have lots of history to offer you.

Letter I is for Industry,
coal and salt and even trees—
fuel to keep us nice and warm
and provide safe shelter from the storm.

Industry in West Virginia makes use of the many natural resources available.

The coal industry has been an important part of the state's economy and its history. In the early 1900s many immigrants came to the United States and found jobs in the coal mines. Working underground with the possibility of explosions or getting black lung disease caused by breathing in coal dust were just a few of the dangers of mining. Mary "Mother" Jones helped to fight for improved working conditions for the miners who often risked their lives and health.

Mining is not limited to coal. The mining industry also produces salt that can be used to make glass and plastic.

Chemical manufacturing plants, like those near Nitro, West Virginia, make use of the natural gas found in the region.

The lumber industry supplies the wood for many things such as building supplies for homes, and paper for making books.

Anna Jarvis was born in Grafton, West Virginia. She is credited with establishing what our nation now celebrates as Mother's Day. Her own mother was known to organize "Mothers' Friendship Day" after the Civil War to bring families from both the Union and the Confederacy together. President Woodrow Wilson's 1914 proclamation urged national recognition of the second Sunday in May each year as Mother's Day. This all began when Anna Jarvis honored her own mother's memory on May 10, 1908 sending 1,000 carnations to a church service. That church, Andrews Methodist Church in Grafton, is now the International Mother's Day Shrine.

Jj

Anna Jarvis helps us celebrate
She honored her mom on a special day.
And now throughout the entire land,
we tell our mothers we think they're grand.

Kanawha is a Native American word that translates to "place of the white stone." The white stone may describe the many salt deposits discovered in the Kanawha Valley. For a few months, Kanawha was the name for the land that would officially become known as West Virginia. The name Kanawha was used for many of the places and features of the state. For example, the Kanawha River runs through several counties including Kanawha County. The town of Kanawha Head is located near the Little Kanawha River. A state forest near Charleston also shares the name Kanawha.

Not every word you read is an easy word to say.
Kanawha, for example, is the word for letter K.
A valley, a river, and a county too
all called Kanawha, just to name a few.

A landmark's lost but can be found.
Look above and below the ground.
Find Lost World Caverns, Lewisburg, and letter L.
They're located near each other, as you can tell.

Lost World Caverns are a registered national landmark full of stalagmites and stalactites. Stalagmites are cave formations that come up from the floor of the cave. Stalactites come down from the cave's ceiling.

(It's easy to remember the difference if you think of the word with the "m" as having "more on the floor." The word with the "t" in place of the "m" defines the ones that come down from the "top.")

Near the Lost World Caverns in the southeastern part of the state you'll find the city of Lewisburg. Its historic Old Stone Church, built in 1796, is made from limestone from the region. Many other buildings date back to the eighteenth and nineteenth century. Some of these buildings show evidence of Civil War battles fought in Lewisburg.

60

64

Lost World
Caverns

Lewisburg

Greenbriar
River

219

VIRGINIA

WEST VIRGINIA

Ll

M m

M may appear like Mountains—
peaks reaching for the sky.
Our nickname is the Mountain State.
It's easy to see why.

The official nickname of West Virginia is Mountain State. A few large valleys along the Ohio and Kanawha rivers are outnumbered by the many mountain ranges.

The Allegheny Mountains were formed years ago by layers and layers of deposits known as sedimentary rock. The Blue Ridge Mountains in the Eastern Panhandle contain igneous and metamorphic rock. Igneous rocks are formed during the cooling off of hot substances. Metamorphic rock is a result of pressure and very high temperatures. The Allegheny and Blue Ridge Mountains are part of a larger range known as the Appalachian Mountains.

With a multitude of mountains West Virginia is a popular skiing destination during the winter months and a favorite spot for many outdoor activities throughout the year.

N n

Wondering if there's life on Mars
or anywhere among the stars?
Visit this place that begins with N,
with great frequency return again.

National Radio Astronomy Observatory, an impressive name for an important destination for scientists and visitors from across the globe.

Located on a mountaintop in Green Bank, West Virginia, the National Radio Astronomy Observatory houses huge radio telescopes that scan outer space for radio waves. Planets, comets, and other objects in space send out radio waves that can be studied by astronomers and other scientists. The National Radio Astronomy Observatory has been in operation since 1959.

Olympian Mary Lou Retton, born in Fairmont, West Virginia, brought home the gold, silver, and bronze from the 1984 Olympic Games. She was the first American woman to win a gold medal in the all-around event. A silver medal in the vault and bronze medals in both the floor exercise and uneven bars added up to four individual medals. Her gymnastics team won the silver medal, bringing her total to five. Mary Lou Retton left the Olympics in Los Angeles with more medals than any other athlete. Her winning smile brightened the front of Wheaties cereal boxes and the Associated Press proclaimed her 1984's "Amateur Athlete of the Year." Mary Lou Retton was also named "Sportswoman of the Year" by *Sports Illustrated* in the same year.

Olympic athlete, an all-around O.
Mary Lou Retton sure put on a show.
The smiling gymnast made us stand and cheer.
1984 was certainly her year!

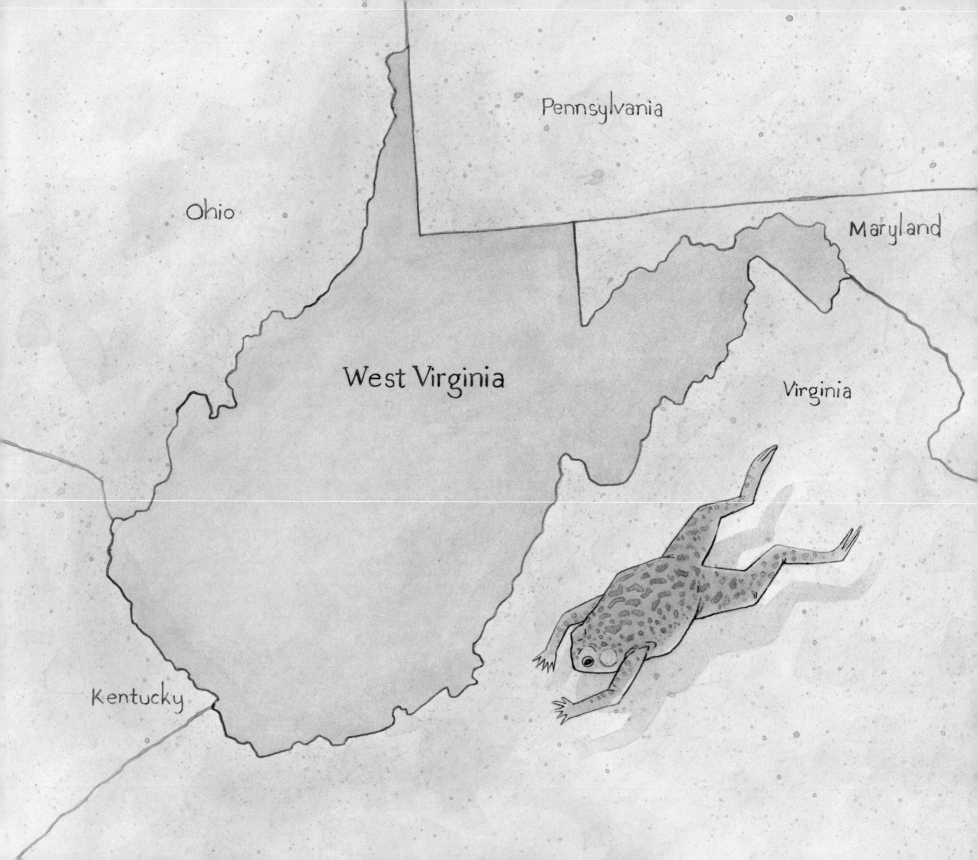

New Jersey

Atlantic Ocean

Delaware

Presenting a page with plenty of **P**s
and the only state with two of these.
Panhandles that is, both north and east
make unique boundaries, to say the least.

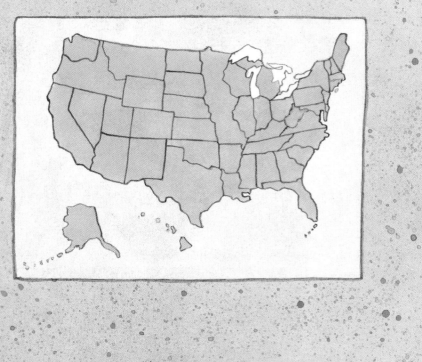

Panhandles are narrow strips of land
that extend beyond the main land area
looking somewhat like the handle of a
pan. West Virginia is the only state in
the country with two panhandles.

The Northern Panhandle is bordered by
Ohio and Pennsylvania. The panhandle
is so narrow that the town of Weirton
touches both of those neighboring
states. The Eastern Panhandle lies
between Maryland and Virginia. Charles
Town, named for George Washington's
youngest brother, is located there.

The panhandles and other natural
boundaries give West Virginia a shape
that is easy to identify on a map. Some
people say it looks like a frog with the
panhandles as its legs kicking out
behind it. What do you think?

Quilting bees have long been an opportunity for socializing and for creating beautiful works of art. Pioneers to present-day quilters have gathered together to stitch fabric pieces into intricately patterned quilts.

Quilt patterns can tell a story or symbolize a special occasion. Many new brides were given a handmade quilt as a gift from the members of their community. Work on the quilt would be started upon the announcement of the engagement and later presented when the couple's home was ready to be furnished.

Not all quilts have distinct patterns. Some quilts were patched together using pieces of fabric in random designs. These were called "Crazy Patch" quilts. They were practical and economical. Fabric was valuable and scraps were not wasted. Neighbors even exchanged pieces of cloth to add variety to their quilts. Warm and interesting quilts resulted when every bit of the scrap was used.

Did you think that you would see
a quilt or perhaps a quilting bee?
Seems as if you always knew
Quilts would represent the letter Q.

Rr

Rafting on the New, Gauley, or one of the other rivers of West Virginia is sure to be a thrill. Rapids offer whitewater excitement at many different skill levels from beginner to expert. World Rafting Championships have been hosted in West Virginia.

Rising nearly 900 feet above the rapids of the New River is the New River Gorge Bridge. It is the second highest bridge in the United States. The Royal Gorge Bridge in Colorado is the only one higher.

Rivers throughout the state have been important for transporting materials and establishing industrial centers along their banks. Wheeling's location on the banks of the Ohio River made it easier to transport items such as wool to other cities. Now it's more likely to be steel from Wheeling that is moved along the rivers.

Rafting on rivers brings us rapidly to R.
With so many rivers, you can travel far.
We can use them for fun and for recreation.
Rivers are also important for transportation.

Though it may sound like many rocks, Seneca Rocks refers to one of the most recognized land formations in the state. Made of lightly colored Tuscarora sandstone, Seneca Rocks stands out among the surrounding landscape. Almost a thousand feet tall, these cliffs are scaled by expert rock climbers. During the early 1940s the United States Army trained its mountain troops at Seneca Rocks.

S s

Strong and solid, you wouldn't expect less
from the sturdy letter S.
Seneca Rocks stands proud and tall,
nature's very own climbing wall.

Trees not only provide shade and shelter, some also provide us with food to eat. Fruit from the apple tree can be delicious. In fact, a specific type of apple, a yellowish apple called Golden Delicious, was discovered in Clay County. In 1995 that variety of apple, Golden Delicious, became the official state fruit, replacing the plain apple.

The sugar maple tree is a source for sweet maple syrup and wood for fine furniture. Autumn showcases the beautiful colors of the sugar maple's leaves. The sugar maple tree has been the official tree of West Virginia since 1949.

Trees that give us lots of wood.
Trees with apples that are oh, so good!
Trees with names that sound so sweet T a special treat.
make letter  a special treat.

T t

Now it's time to take a turn.
Letter **U** for places to learn.
Universities are a place to cheer,
especially when you're a Mountaineer.

Universities and colleges throughout West Virginia are sources of pride and tradition. Bethany College was established in 1840 and is the oldest college in the state. Marshall University in Huntington is named in honor of John Marshall, Chief Justice of the Supreme Court from 1801 to 1835.

The largest university is West Virginia University in Morgantown. Mountaineer spirit comes alive in a special way when crowds gather to cheer on the sports teams. Though the state has no professional teams, athletes from these schools have gone on to play professional sports. Sam Huff and Jerry West both attended West Virginia University. Huff entered the Professional Football Hall of Fame in 1982 after playing for the New York Giants and Washington Redskins. Jerry West received all-American honors at WVU and played basketball for the Los Angeles Lakers before becoming their head coach.

Vandalia Gathering for letter V—
a celebration filled with glee.
Music and dancing and lots of fun,
something to enjoy for everyone.

The term "Vandalia" has come to represent the yearning for freedom in the mountains. The Vandalia Gathering celebrates the culture and heritage of West Virginians who cherish that freedom.

Musicians, dancers, folk artists, and storytellers join together annually on the grounds of the state capitol to share their talents and pass on their traditions. Appalachian fiddlers and Native American dancers are just a few of the performers who entertain as they educate those who gather in Charleston each May.

What in the world could be better for you
than a visit with wonderful W?
Welcome to West Virginia's White Sulphur Springs,
a place to relax and enjoy many things.

White Sulphur Springs is one of many towns named for mineral springs nearby. The mineral springs were known for their health benefits. These springs have attracted visitors for many decades. The Old White Hotel, now known as The Greenbrier, hosted Presidents Van Buren, Tyler, and Fillmore. White Sulphur Springs provided a lovely location, away from the hustle and bustle of the nation's capital.

Golfers have also been attracted to White Sulphur Springs. One of the first golf courses in America, Oakhurst Links, dates back to 1884. The first match on the course was postponed several weeks because golf clubs sent from Scotland were confiscated by customs inspectors. They thought that the clubs looked like dangerous weapons. The inspectors were unfamiliar with the new game called golf.

Steam powered locomotives and flat cars were used to transport lumber to the mill in the town of Cass, West Virginia in the early 1900s. At the height of production, loggers cut over a million feet of lumber per week. The logging camps are preserved today in Cass Scenic Railroad State Park located in Pocahontas County. You can board the historic trains and travel a very steep grade of 11 feet in altitude for each 100 feet of track. The steam locomotives must stop and take on more water to produce enough steam to make the trip all of the way up to Bald Knob. With an altitude more than 4,000 feet, it is the second highest place in the state.

Railroads have played an important part in the history and economy of West Virginia.

Industries depending on natural resources also depended on the railroads to deliver those materials. The geography of the state made construction of railways difficult, but as tunnels were drilled through the mountains new areas of the state were able to be developed. Huntington, Elkins, and Davis are cities named for influential railroaders.

Xx

Letter X lets you know
you're near a place a train might go.
Excitement builds as locomotives climb
up steep hills and back in time.

Y y

Soaring high up in the sky
is where we find the letter Y.
And Chuck Yeager could be found
flying faster than the speed of sound.

The first person to ever fly faster than the speed of sound was Brigadier General Charles Yeager. In 1947, less than 50 years after the Wright brothers made aviation history flying at a speed of 31 miles per hour, Chuck Yeager piloted a rocket-powered Bell-X-1 faster than the speed of sound. A native of Myra, West Virginia, Yeager continued to break records. In 1953 he flew two and one-half times the speed of sound.

Yeager Airport in Charleston is named in his honor.

Zenith, meaning "the top, highest point, the summit," seems an appropriate word for letter Z and the Mountain State.

Zenith is also the name of a town in the southeastern part of the state. On a mountaintop near Zenith is Hanging Rock Observatory, a former fire observation post for the Jefferson National Forest. The observatory is now used to study the migration of eagles, falcons, hawks, and other birds. With an elevation of 3,800 feet, it's a perfect place to take in the spectacular scenery and views of West Virginia.

Sum it up with Zenith, the mountain's very top.
Letter Z seems to be a very good place to stop.
From here we can see from A to Z an almost heavenly view,
and the inspiring beauty that West Virginia offers you.

A Valley Full of Facts

1. What is the state animal of West Virginia?

2. How many panhandles shape the state of West Virginia?

3. What is the state capital of West Virginia?

4. What color is the capitol dome?

5. Name the first person to fly faster than the speed of sound.

6. What is the state bird of West Virginia?

7. What is the largest Adena burial mound in West Virginia?

8. What is the highest point in West Virginia?

9. What is the state fish of West Virginia?

10. What is the state motto of West Virginia?

11. Where was award-winning author Pearl S. Buck born?

12. Name two natural resources mined in West Virginia.

13. How many medals did gymnast Mary Lou Retton win at the 1984 Olympics?

14. What is the official state fruit of West Virginia?

15. What powered the locomotives used at the logging camps in the early 1900s?

16. Name the First Lady who helped West Virginians find housing during the Great Depression of the 1930s.

17. What year did West Virginia become the 35th state?

18. What is the official nickname of West Virginia?

Answers

1. Black bear
2. Two
3. Charleston
4. Gold
5. Charles (Chuck) Yeager
6. cardinal
7. Grave Creek Mound
8. Spruce Knob
9. brook trout
10. *"Montani Semper Liberi,"*
   "Mountaineers Are Always Free"

11. Hillsboro, West Virginia
12. coal, salt
13. five total, 1 team and 4 individual medals
14. Golden Delicious apple
15. steam
16. Eleanor Roosevelt
17. 1863
18. Mountain State

Mary Ann McCabe Riehle

Mary Ann McCabe Riehle learned to appreciate the importance of reading and writing while growing up in the neighboring state of Kentucky. She graduated from Xavier University with a degree in communication arts and education. Mary Ann has been a featured author and guest speaker at reading, writing, and library conferences. *B is for Bluegrass: A Kentucky Alphabet* was her first children's book and she is pleased to follow it up with *M is for Mountain State: A West Virginia Alphabet*.

Mary Ann lives in Michigan with her husband, two daughters, and their dog, Bisbee. Though she has traveled extensively she believes that there is no place more beautiful than our United States. West Virginia certainly showcases that beauty.

Laura J. Bryant

Laura J. Bryant attended the Maryland Institute of Art where she received a strong foundation in drawing, painting, and printmaking. She spent many years working for companies within the display industry which involved both illustrating and designing scenery for stage backdrops, corporate galas, political events, and conventions. She currently devotes all of her attention to the creation of children's books. Laura's other titles include *A Fairy in a Dairy*, *Smudge Bunny*, and the best-selling book *God Gave Us You*.

Laura and her husband are nestled among the Shenandoah Mountains in Mathias, West Virginia where they have restored an old farmhouse and enjoy the company of their cat, Paco.